Slippery BABIES

YOUNG FROGS, TOADS, AND SALAMANDERS

GINNY JOHNSTON

Slippery
BABIES

YOUNG FROGS, TOADS,
AND SALAMANDERS

JUDY CUTCHINS

MORROW JUNIOR BOOKS
NEW YORK

PHOTO CREDITS

Permission for the following photographs is gratefully acknowledged: Animals, Animals © 1991 Michael Fogden, pp. 13–15; Ted Borg, p. 21; Fernbank Science Center, pp. 3, 26; George Grall, p. 7; Tom Tyning, pp. 10, 11; Lawrence A. Wilson, pp. 2, 4, 19, 31, 35. All other photographs by Judy Cutchins.

The text type is 14 point Meridien.
Book design by Karen Palinko.

1 2 3 4 5 6 7 8 9 10

Library of Congress Cataloging-in-Publication Data
Johnston, Ginny.
Slippery babies : young frogs, toads, and salamanders /
Ginny Johnston, Judy Cutchins.
p.   cm.
Includes index.
Summary: Describes the physical characteristics and behavior of a variety of baby amphibians as they struggle to survive and grow to maturity.
ISBN 0-688-09605-0 (trade). — ISBN 0-688-09606-9 (library)
1. Amphibians—Development—Juvenile literature.   [1. Amphibians.
2. Animals—Infancy.]   I. Cutchins, Judy.   II. Title.
QL644.2.C87 1991
597.6'0439—dc20
90-49665 CIP AC

Acknowledgments

We wish to thank the following specialists for their help in ensuring the accuracy of *Slippery Babies*: Jack Cover, Assistant Rain Forest Curator, National Aquarium, Baltimore, Maryland; Dennis Herman, Assistant Reptile Curator, Zoo Atlanta, Atlanta, Georgia; Thomas F. Tyning, Master Naturalist, Massachusetts Audubon Society, Lenox, Massachusetts; Lawrence A. Wilson, Herpetologist, Fernbank Science Center, Atlanta, Georgia. We also wish to express our appreciation to Fernbank Science Center, Ted Borg, George Grall, Tom Tyning, and Larry Wilson for the use of their outstanding photographs.

Contents

Amphibians and Their Babies

O ver 350 different kinds of salamanders exist in the world today, and ten times that many types of frogs and toads. There is tremendous variety among these almost four thousand kinds of amphibians. Many have not been well studied by scientists, so some of their habits remain unknown.

In spite of the variety, amphibians have certain things in common. One characteristic is that amphibians are dependent on moist or even wet habitats throughout their lives. Although the sun provides needed warmth for these cold-blooded animals, they cannot stay in the hot, drying sun too long. Every kind of amphibian, no matter where it lives, must keep its tender, thin skin moist throughout its life. This is why amphibians often look and feel slippery.

Skin is more than just a body covering for an amphibian. These animals drink and breathe through their skin. As long as their skin is moist,

The slippery skin of a Monterey salamander is thin and moist. The salamander protects its skin from drying out by hiding under damp moss and leaves in its woodland habitat.

amphibians can absorb oxygen directly into tiny blood vessels. Their skin also absorbs the water they need, so most amphibians do not drink.

Amphibians lay their eggs in ponds, pools, or damp places. The eggs do not have hard shells like those of birds. Instead, each egg has a clear, jellylike covering around it. The jelly swells after the eggs are laid, and the eggs often stick to one another or to plants underwater. This transparent covering allows sunshine to incubate each egg so the animal will develop inside. Hatching occurs when a baby becomes large and active enough to wriggle free.

This salamander egg will soon hatch and the larva will be on its own. No parent salamander will take care of it.

Hatchling amphibians, called larvae, usually do not look like their parents. Larvae have gills and breathe like fish. They also have flattened tails that help them swim in their watery nursery. As they become older, larvae grow legs and lose their gills. Frog and toad youngsters lose their tails, while salamanders keep long tails throughout their lives. Undergoing

A frog's large, flat eardrums are located just behind its eyes. Excellent hearing helps many amphibians escape from predators.

such changes in body form is called metamorphosis. It may be days, months, or sometimes years before a baby amphibian completes its metamorphosis and resembles its parents.

During its early life, a baby amphibian is on its own. In only a few cases does a parent take care of an egg or larva. However, a newly hatched amphibian does not have to be taught how to protect itself or find food. Each has instincts for survival and needs little or no help from a parent.

Amphibians play important roles in the food chains of their habitats. They eat tremendous numbers of insects, slugs, worms, and other small animals. In turn, amphibians are eaten by birds, snakes, fish, and mammals, helping to keep nature in balance.

Because amphibians are small and have delicate skin, many adults as well as young ones do not survive the hazards in their lives. Dry, hot weather can be extremely dangerous to a frog, toad, or salamander. When amphibians escape from predators, it is often because of their secretive habits and their protective adaptations.

Slippery Babies: Young Frogs, Toads, and Salamanders describes the variety of ways some amphibians develop, grow, and survive. Their stories are a sampling of the amazing diversity in the amphibian world.

ONE

Baby Frogs

Frogs are perhaps the best jumpers in the world, and many are excellent swimmers. Their legs are muscular, and their bodies are sleek and streamlined. In North America, frogs vary in size from the eight-inch-long bullfrog to the half-inch-long little grass frog.

Most frog eggs are laid in quiet, shallow water. Often hundreds, even thousands, of eggs float in clumps on the water's surface. Frog hatchlings, or larvae, are called tadpoles. A tadpole eats by using its beaklike mouth to scrape algae from rocks or plants in the water. As a tadpole goes through metamorphosis, its tail gradually shrinks. This happens because the nourishment that is stored in the tail is used up by the larva as it changes. When a little froglet leaves the water, often just a stump of its tail remains.

Once a froglet's mouth develops a wide, "grinning" shape, the baby frog can eat insects. Its long, sticky tongue flicks out to catch prey. The frog's tongue is fastened at the front of its mouth rather than at the back like a human's tongue. So when the frog's tongue darts back in, the insect is flipped into the throat, where it is easily swallowed.

It will be several years before a froglet is fully grown and ready to seek a mate. Adult male frogs call in the early springtime to attract females. The chorus of voices sounds as if the frogs are answering one another, but they are not. Each male is trying to outsing his neighbors. When a female approaches, a male will clasp her body, piggyback style, in the water. As she lays her eggs, the male releases his sperm to fertilize them. Most frogs abandon their eggs, but some guard them and even care for the tadpoles when they hatch.

Each male wood frog fertilizes a female's eggs as she lays them in the shallow water. On a winter evening, dozens of wood frogs may be found in one pond.

~Bullfrog~

Sunny spring days have gradually warmed the dark water of Georgia's Okefenokee Swamp. A bullfrog tadpole flutters its tail and swims away from the muddy bottom. During the winter, the tadpole had barely moved. Its chilled body used little energy and needed no food. But as the swamp water warms, the tadpole becomes more active. Its strong, flat tail swishes back and forth as the little amphibian swims toward an algae-covered log. The tadpole scrapes off its first meal of the spring.

The bullfrog tadpole is a year old. This youngster is one of the lucky few that hatched and survived from a softball-sized mass of more than five thousand eggs. Many of the hatchlings were eaten by crayfish, water insects, snakes, turtles, or fish.

A giant water bug preys on small animals such as tadpoles and froglets.

This froglet has developed front and back legs. Soon its shrinking tail will completely disappear.

Bullfrog tadpoles are the largest kind of tadpoles in the United States. Last year the half-inch-long tadpole grew to be almost three inches long. This spring it will grow bigger before beginning its metamorphosis.

First, both tiny back legs with their webbed feet will push through the skin on either side of its tail. A few weeks after that, the right front leg will push out of the tadpole's body. Then, a few days later, its left leg will appear.

Besides the growing of legs, many other amazing changes will occur in the bullfrog tadpole. Its bladelike tail will get shorter as the fat stored in it is used by the changing larva. Its small, round eyes will move to the top of its head and bulge outward. These amazing eyes are especially adapted for spotting anything that moves and is small enough to swallow. Each eye will develop top and bottom eyelids that are the color of the skin. A third eyelid, called a nictitating membrane, will form beneath the bottom eyelid. This thin, clear layer of skin closes over each eyeball whenever a frog dives underwater. Frogs have excellent vision while swimming because the nictitating membranes act like a pair of swim goggles.

The nictitating membrane closes to protect the frog's eye underwater.

A tadpole breathes through gills, which are inside its body. As the larva changes into a frog, lungs and nostrils take over part of the job of breathing. The young bullfrog can come to the surface for air, but it does not have to. A bullfrog, like all amphibians, can absorb oxygen from air or water directly through its thin, moist skin. Oxygen passes into the blood vessels that are near the skin's surface. Skin-breathing makes it possible for a frog to bury itself in mud for the winter or stay underwater for a long time.

By late summer, the froglet will spend most of its time on the marshy bank. Raccoons, otters, and snakes searching the leaf litter and shallow water are a serious danger for the young frog. But an alert bullfrog is an escape artist. If a shadow crosses its body, the startled frog squawks and

Quiet and camouflaged, a young bullfrog watches for prey as well as for danger. Even a shadow will send the bullfrog diving to the bottom to hide.

leaps into deep water, where it hides on the bottom. In the water, the froglet could become prey for a hungry snapping turtle, fish, or young alligator. Luckily, the bullfrog is also a speedy swimmer.

On a diet of insects, the youngster will grow to be as long as a man's hand by the time it is three years old. For the rest of its ten- to twelve-year life, the bullfrog will never leave the edge of the swamp.

Bullfrogs are found in North America east of the Rocky Mountains.

~ Poison Dart Frog ~

Two frogs push and shove as they wrestle high up in a Central American rain forest. Each male strawberry poison dart frog is battling to claim the tree as his territory. After several minutes of fighting, the smaller frog leaps away. The winner chirps loudly. He will now try to attract a female. His throat swells out like a balloon as his mating calls ring out through the

The fight between males will determine which one claims this tree as his territory.

rain forest. In the jungle, where it is humid and warm year-round, poison dart frogs mate and lay eggs during any month of the year.

When a female approaches, the two begin a courtship dance. They circle each other, bow, and hug. After courtship, a female will lay up to a dozen eggs in the damp leaf litter on the jungle floor. Like many amphibians in tropical forests, strawberry poison dart frogs do not deposit their eggs in a pond or stream. After the female lays her eggs, the male climbs on top of them. He releases his sperm to fertilize the tiny eggs.

This inch-long male strawberry poison dart frog makes his mating call by pumping air back and forth between his mouth and lungs. A balloonlike vocal sac swells out and makes the sound louder.

For two weeks, the female watches over her eggs. Occasionally she urinates on them to keep them moist. As the eggs hatch, the mother frog backs up to her tadpoles and allows one to wiggle up onto her back. Sticky mucus on the surface of her skin keeps the tadpole from sliding off.

With acrobatic ease, the female climbs into a tree. On a branch high off the ground, she finds a plant called a bromeliad. These unusual plants grow on tree trunks and branches throughout the rain forest. Their thick, waxy leaves fit snugly together and form a cup that holds rainwater. When the poison dart frog finds a bromeliad, she steps backward into the

The mother poison dart frog carries each tadpole, one at a time, to a pool of water in the center of a bromeliad plant.

pool of water. The water loosens the sticky mucus, and the piggyback-riding tadpole slides off into its nursery pool. The mother then returns to the ground and taxis the next baby to a different bromeliad.

Every few days, the mother frog visits her larvae. Backing into each pool, she releases an unfertilized egg for her youngster to eat. The infertile egg has a nutritious yolk but no developing tadpole inside. Most of the babies survive the tadpole stage because of their mother's special attention.

When a strawberry poison dart tadpole completes its metamorphosis, it hops from the bromeliad nursery. It makes its way down the tree to the jungle floor. Here it will live the rest of its life, finding shelter and insects for food in the leaf litter.

The young frog's skin is bright and colorful like that of the adults. Newly developed mucous glands make the froglet shiny and moist. It now has glands in the skin that secrete a powerful toxin. The toxin is a deadly poison to most biting predators. Brilliant colors, which make the froglet so easy to see, warn enemies to stay away. While the poison dart frog's predators are few, some spiders and snakes are not affected by the toxin and feed on these beautiful little animals.

Poison dart frogs can be seen in rain forests of South and Central America.

Baby Toads

W arty bodies and funny, awkward hops make many toads easy to identify. These plump creatures are rarely seen because they hide all day and hunt at night. Smart gardeners know that toads are helpful because they eat caterpillars, beetles, slugs, and other pests. Thousands of insects disappear from a garden each summer evening, thanks to the toads.

Because toads often live far from ponds, females may lay thousands of eggs in shallow puddles or in roadside rain ditches. Most toad eggs are laid in long strings and look like necklaces of beads. Tremendous numbers of eggs never hatch because puddles often dry up too fast in the summer's heat. If the warm water remains, a tiny, black tadpole may hatch in just a few days. In about two months, a toad tadpole may complete its metamorphosis in the same way a frog does.

Toads cannot leap fast or far to escape from predators. Tiny toadlets rely

Female toads lay thousands of eggs in long strings that look like strands of tiny black pearls.

on hiding and camouflage to avoid birds, lizards, and baby snakes that might eat them.

As a toadlet grows, its smooth skin becomes rough with warty-looking bumps. Behind each eye, a large parotoid gland develops. These egg-shaped glands secrete a milky toxin that burns the mouth of most animals that try to eat the toad. A fox might grab a toad and immediately spit it out. While the toad may not survive such a bite, the fox will soon learn not to bite toads. Contrary to popular belief, touching either the toxin or the toad's skin does not cause warts to grow on people.

From the oval glands behind each eye, this American toad secretes a bitter-tasting toxin. Predators quickly learn to avoid toads and find another meal.

~ Southern Toad ~

It is nearly midnight at a Florida roadside pond. A tiny toadlet kicks its way to the water's edge and climbs out for the first time. It rests on the muddy bank before beginning life on land. The toadlet is not alone. Hundreds and hundreds of new southern toads are hopping off in every direction.

Toad tadpoles crowd a shallow Florida pond, gobbling algae with their scraper-like mouths.

Pine needles along the pond bank make hopping difficult for these new, half-inch-long toadlets.

A mosquito flies close to the toadlet and disappears. The young toad's sticky tongue flicks out faster than a human eye can see. Anything that moves and is small enough to swallow will be food for the hungry little hunter. The toad's throat moves in and out constantly as it breathes the warm night air. Its shiny, golden eyes search for another meal.

With each hop, the half-inch-long toadlet moves about an inch. It will not travel far from the pond this first night. Before the sun comes up, the toadlet will dig into the soft soil. Spurs on its back feet work like little shovels, and soon the toad disappears, backward, into the hole it has made. When it is buried in the damp soil, the toad's thin skin will not dry out. Oxygen between the soil particles will be absorbed through the toad's skin. Hiding is also the best way for the toadlet to avoid being eaten by crows or snakes.

The toxin secreted by glands in a toad's skin works well to protect it from birds, foxes, and many other enemies. One animal that is not bothered by the toxin, however, is the hognose snake. In fact, these snakes eat almost nothing but toads. However, a toad has an unusual way of defending itself against a hognose. The toad gulps air into its stomach and intestines and blows up like a balloon. Because a snake eats its prey whole, a puffed-up toad might be too big for the snake to swallow. Once the snake has slithered away, the toad slowly returns to its normal size.

A few nights after leaving the pond, the little southern toad may hop into a backyard garden. For twenty or thirty years, this same insect-filled place could be its home. Soon the growing toadlet will need to shed its old skin. A new layer will form beneath the top layer. The worn-out outer layer then loosens and splits in several places. The little toad will twist and tear this layer off in strips. Balling up the old skin with its front feet, the toadlet will swallow the bundle. It contains valuable nutrients important in the toad's diet. Shedding takes only five minutes, and a fast-growing toadlet may shed every week. During this first summer, the little toad will more than double in size. After six weeks on land, it will be one inch long. Like all amphibians, toads will continue to shed and eat their skins throughout their lives.

As the toad grows, it can swallow larger prey. Earthworms become a favorite food. Stepping slowly, one foot at a time, the toad will stalk around a long worm. Soon the two are head to head. Lightning-fast, the toad's sticky tongue lashes out. It sticks to the earthworm and brings the worm's head into the toad's mouth. The little toad uses its front feet to stuff the worm down its throat.

In three or four years, the toadlet will be three inches long and fully grown. Each year, the toad will disappear for a few days in early spring. It will hop toward nearby water, find a mate, and begin another generation of southern toadlets.

Southern toads are found in the coastal plain from Virginia to Louisiana.

The high-pitched mating call of a male toad is heard on warm spring evenings, especially after a rain.

THREE

Baby Salamanders

Shy, secretive salamanders are rarely seen during the day. Most remain hidden underground, where they are safe from predators and from the drying sun. At night, they move about in search of small prey. On an unusually warm, rainy night in late winter, thousands of salamanders may be seen marching in the woods. They are adults of many kinds, heading for nearby water to mate and lay eggs. Some return to the place where they hatched several years before.

Males deposit spermatophores, packets of sperm, in the shallow water or near the water's edge. By following a scent trail that the male leaves, a female salamander finds some of the sperm packets left by males of her same kind. Already plump with eggs, she rubs across several spermatophores, taking the sperm into her body through an opening beneath her tail. Sperm fertilize her eggs just before they are laid. Although there are exceptions, most salamanders lay small clusters of eggs, or even individual eggs, in the water. They often place them on a twig, leaf, or stem of a water plant.

Over several nights, a male spotted salamander may deposit as many as one hundred of these spermatophores, or sperm capsules, in a breeding pool.

Depending on the temperature of the water, eggs will hatch in a few weeks. As with most amphibians, colder temperatures slow down development, while warmer ones cause the eggs to hatch more quickly. For a few days after hatching, many kinds of salamander larvae have small, rodlike growths called balancers near their jaws. These help the babies balance until their legs grow longer.

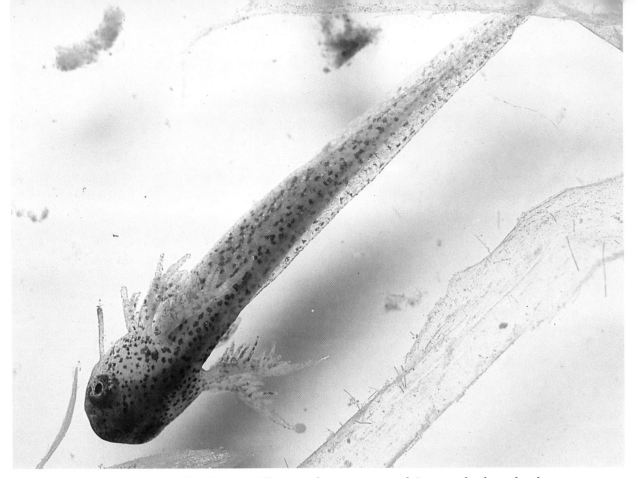

Rodlike balancers and feathery gills can be seen on this newly hatched salamander.

A hatchling salamander has a thin, flat tail. As the youngster grows, its tail becomes thicker and rounder. A salamander larva, unlike frog and toad tadpoles, does not lose its tail as it goes through metamorphosis.

Amphibian larvae usually breathe with gills. At hatching, gills are outside an amphibian's body. While frog and toad gills are soon covered by flaps of skin, the larval salamander's gills remain outside. Most salamanders lose their feathery gills during metamorphosis and begin their life on land. Some kinds keep their gills, even as adults, and remain in water all their lives.

～ Spotted Salamander ～

Water trickled down a New England mountainside as warm April temperatures melted the winter ice. In a forest near the foot of the mountain, the cold water slowed and formed a wide, shallow pool. In a few days, the pool was dotted with clear clusters of spotted salamander eggs. Hungry raccoons, crows, and snakes ate many of the eggs.

As the water gradually warmed, green algae grew around each of the eggs that remained. The algae produced oxygen needed for the developing larvae to live. Inside its jellylike covering, each baby developed feathery gills, a broad tail, and the beginnings of front legs.

Every other year, a female spotted salamander lays about 150 eggs. The eggs soon swell to a softball-sized mass.

Now, just six weeks after the eggs were laid, young spotted salamanders are hatching. A tiny larva clings to the jelly mass for support. In a short time, the front legs will become useful for balancing, and the baby amphibian will swim on its own. Throughout the spring and early summer, all the larvae will remain in the pool. They will find shelter and food in the leaves and pine needles on the bottom.

As weeks go by, the larva needs more food as its body rapidly grows. It becomes a small but fierce predator, hunting anything in the water that moves. The larva sees and smells wiggling worms and water insects. Moving cautiously, like a stalking cat, the baby spotted salamander gets close enough to pounce. In a flash, the larva's wide mouth opens and a bite-sized prey is sucked inside. Off the baby salamander goes in search of more food.

With so many larvae searching the pool for food, it is not surprising that one occasionally bites off the leg or the tail of another. Amazingly, the injured larva will make a complete recovery. Both larvae and adult salamanders can regrow, or regenerate, missing body parts. All amphibians have this extraordinary adaptation to some degree.

Within eight weeks, this larval salamander will regenerate its missing foot. This unusual adaptation of regrowing body parts helps many amphibians survive attacks from predators.

By June, the larval spotted salamander's gills will disappear. Its metamorphosis will be complete. The salamander will be the size of a person's little finger when the amphibian leaves its underwater life forever. In three years, it will grow to a length of eight inches.

Nosing and digging into damp soil and leaves, the spotted salamander will remain hidden for much of its twenty- or thirty-year lifetime. With luck, the beautiful spotted salamander will not be eaten by a raccoon, opossum, or other nighttime predator.

Spotted salamanders can be seen all over the eastern United States and even in parts of southern Canada.

Secretive and shy, the spotted salamander ventures out of its hiding place only at night to search for food.

～Red-Spotted Newt～

The summer afternoon is cool and damp, just right for a hunting salamander. Moving its head from side to side, the three-inch-long salamander stalks a beetle on the forest floor. These amphibians are well known for their great appetites. Snails, slugs, millipedes, and spiders are all possible prey.

The salamander hatched in a quiet forest pond. When the larva's body changed, its name changed, too. The larval red-spotted newt in the pond became a red eft living in the woods.

No bigger than a small marble, each red-spotted newt egg is hidden among the water plants.

The red eft is the land-living stage of the red-spotted newt.

The little eft's beautiful red skin is different from the skin of most salamanders. It is rough and dry. The bright red color is easy for predators to see. But to many, it is not an invitation to bite—it is a warning. Like the skin of certain other amphibians, the red eft's skin produces a toxin that burns the mouths of most predators. The toxin can even kill small animals. This adaptation makes it possible for the eft to walk about safely during the day. The salamander does have a few enemies, however. Skunks are known to tear red efts apart and eat their insides.

After four years of life in the forest, the red eft's body will begin to change again. Its skin will become smooth and slick instead of rough. It will no longer produce a toxin, and the bright red color will turn greenish brown. The eft's tail will grow broader and flatter for swimming. It will return to the nearby pond where it started life as a larva.

With its body changes completed, the salamander will no longer be called a red eft. For the rest of its life, which may be as long as six more years, it will be known as a red-spotted newt.

After several years on land, the red-spotted newt returns to the water and spends the rest of its life there.

The adult newt will not have gills as it did when it was a larva. Occasionally it will swim to the surface of the pond and gulp a breath of air. But most of the oxygen it needs will be absorbed through the newt's delicate skin.

Each day the four-inch-long salamander will walk along the mucky bottom in search of worms, snails, and water insects. The newt will stalk prey in the water much as it did when it was a red eft on land.

The red-spotted newt has one of the most complicated lives of all amphibians. Throughout its various stages, the newt plays an important role in both pond and woodland food chains. Hundreds of these predators patrol their habitats, feeding on snails, slugs, worms, and any other tiny animals they can catch.

Red-spotted newts are found east of the Mississippi River, as far south as Georgia and Alabama and as far north as southern Canada.

A Future for Baby Amphibians?

Frogs, toads, and salamanders have never been very popular animals. Perhaps it is because they are slippery and slimy. Or maybe it is simply because they are secretive and most people know little about them. Myths, such as the beliefs that toads cause warts or that salamanders can walk through fire, arise from misunderstanding. Of all the major animal groups in the world, amphibians are the least harmful to humans. In fact, they are one of the most beneficial groups of animals.

The role of amphibians in the balance of nature is an important one. By eating insects and other small creatures, amphibians keep the number of these animals from becoming too large. In turn, amphibians are food for hundreds of kinds of larger animals. Scientists know that amphibians are a very important link in most woodland food chains. Even with so many adaptations for survival, it is amazing to discover just how few amphibians ever become adults. Of the thousands of eggs laid by an American toad, for example, perhaps one hundred toadlets survive the first year. Probably no more than ten toadlets live long enough to become adults themselves.

In many parts of the world, amphibians are disappearing altogether. Pollution and the destruction of wetland habitats are making it impossible for them to survive. Declining amphibian populations may indicate that there are serious problems in the environment. These problems affect other kinds of animals, too.

The rare Pine Barrens treefrog lives in swamps and bogs. As these wetland habitats are destroyed, the treefrog loses its living space.

Today more people are concerned about the quality of their environment and the well-being of wildlife. Currently ten kinds of amphibians are protected in the United States by endangered species laws. As humans learn more about the needs of animals and learn how to solve environmental problems, they will greatly improve the chances of a healthy future for all living things.

Glossary

Adaptation—an animal's behavior or a feature of its body that helps the animal survive in its surroundings.

Algae—any of a type of water plant without true roots, stems, or leaves.

Amphibian—any of a group of animals that generally hatch from jelly-coated eggs and go through body changes known as metamorphosis. Many amphibians live in water after hatching. As adults, they live on land.

Cold-blooded—having a body temperature that varies with the surrounding temperature.

Egg—a female reproductive cell.

Fertilize—to unite sperm with eggs for reproduction.

Gills—the breathing organs that take oxygen from water.

Habitat—the place where an animal or plant lives naturally.

Hatchling—an animal that has just emerged from its egg.

Incubate—to warm an egg so the young inside will develop.

Larva (plural: **larvae**)—a newly hatched amphibian.

Leaf litter—dead, fallen leaves that decay to form soil on the forest floor.

Metamorphosis—the change in body structures a larva undergoes to become an adult.

Mucus—the moist, sticky secretion from certain skin glands.

Predator—an animal that kills other animals for food.

Prey—an animal killed and eaten by another animal.

Sperm—a male reproductive cell.

Toxin—a poisonous substance produced by glands in the skin of some amphibians.

Tropical rain forest—a type of forest rich in plant and animal life that stays green year-round owing to high rainfall and warm temperatures; often called a jungle.

Warning coloration—bright colors or patterns on an animal that serve to warn predators to stay away.

Index

Photographs are in **boldface**.